Learn French Verbs with

Odéon Livre
Chicago
2019

Designed by Ethan Safron

Odéon Livre

Chicago, IL USA

On the even side of the book, one will find quotes relating to the featured artwork. English translations of the original French have been set in *italics*.

On the odd side, a verb from the quote will be translated and conjugated in the present form. Again, the English translation of these phrases are written in *italics*.

To find the conjugated verb in its original context, look for a word written in this color.

Ce qui est important, ça
ne se voit pas…

*"The thing that is important is the thing
that is not seen…"*

être	je suis	nous sommes
to be	*I am*	*we are*
	tu es	vous êtes
	you are	*you are*
	il est	ils sont
	he is	*they are*

On ne voit bien qu'avec le cœur.
L'essentiel est invisible pour les yeux.

"It is only with the heart that one can see rightly; what is essential is invisible to the eye."

voir
to see

je vois
I see

nous voyons
we see

tu vois
you see

vous voyez
you see

il voit
he sees

ils voient
they see

Et je suis née en même temps que le soleil…

And I was born at the same moment as the sun…

naître to be born	je nais *I am born*	nous naissons *we are born*
	tu nais *you are born*	vous naissez *you are born*
	il naît *he is born*	ils naissent *they are born*

La planète d'où il venait est
l'astéroïde B-612…

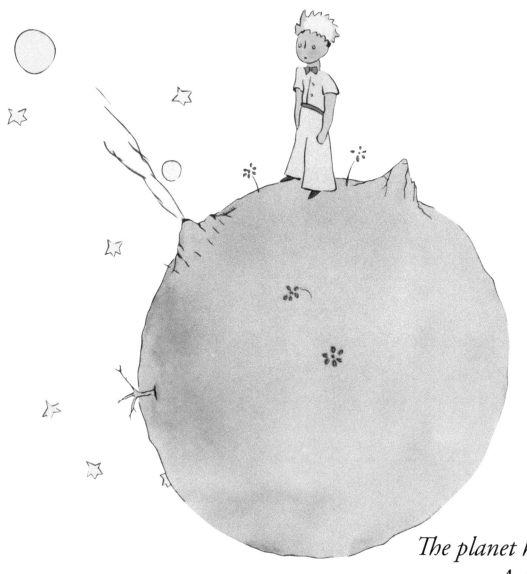

The planet he came from is
Asteroid B-612…

venir to come	je viens *I come*	nous venons *we come*
	tu viens *you come*	vous venez *you come*
	il vient *he comes*	ils viennent *they come*

C'est le temps que tu as
perdu pour ta rose qui fait
ta rose si importante.

*It is the time you have wasted for your
rose that makes your rose so important.*

faire	je fais	nous faisons
to make, to do	*I make*	*we make*
	tu fais	vous faites
	you make	*you make*
	il fait	ils font
	he makes	*they make*

Tu sais… quand on est tellement triste on aime les couchers de soleil…

You know, one loves the sunset, when one is so sad…

aimer to love	j'aime *I love*	nous aimons *we love*
	tu aimes *you love*	vous aimez *you love*
	il aime *he loves*	ils aiment *they love*

Mais à elle seule elle est
plus importante que vous
toutes, puisque c'est elle
que j'ai arrosée.

But in herself alone she is more
important than all the hundreds of
you other roses: because it is she that
I have watered.

arroser to water	j'arrose *I water*	nous arrosons *we water*
	tu arroses *you water*	vous arrosez *you water*
	il arrose *he waters*	ils arrosent *they water*

Les fleurs sont faibles. Elles
sont naïves. Elles se rassurent
comme elles peuvent.
Elles se croient terribles avec
leurs épines…

*"Flowers are weak creatures. They are naïve. They reassure
themselves as best they can. They believe that their thorns
are terrible weapons…"*

croire to believe	je crois *I believe*	nous croyons *we believe*
	tu crois *you believe*	vous croyez *you believe*
	il croit *he believes*	ils croient *they believe*

Si tu réussis à bien te juger, c'est que tu es un véritable sage.

If you succeed in judging yourself rightly, then you are indeed a man of true wisdom.

réussir to succeed	je réussis *I succeed*	nous réussisons *we succeed*
	tu réussis *you succeed*	vous réussissez *you succeed*
	il réussit *he succeeds*	ils réussissent *they succeed*

Le petit prince traversa
le désert et ne rencontra
qu'une fleur.

*The little prince crossed
the desert and encoun-
tered only one flower.*

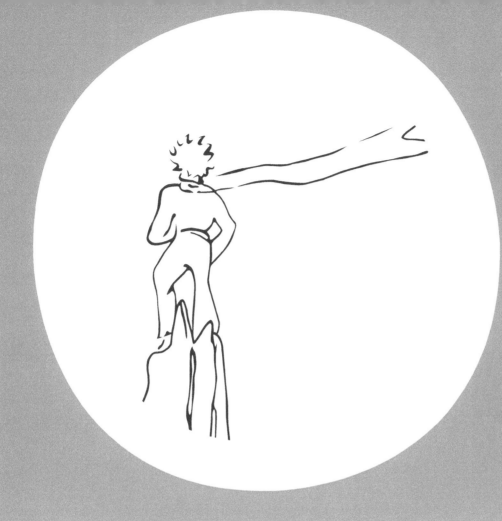

aller	je vais	nous allons
to go	*I go*	*we go*
	tu vas	vous allez
	you go	*you go*
traverser = aller	il va	ils vont
	he goes	*they go*

Ma maison cachait un secret au fond de son cœur…

My home was hiding a secret in the depths of its heart...

cacher
to hide

je cache
I hide

tu caches
you hide

il cache
he hides

nous cachons
we hide

vous cachez
you hide

ils cachent
they hide

Tu entends, dit le petit prince, nous réveillons ce puits et il chante…

"Do you hear?" said the little prince. "We have wakened the well, and it is singing…"

entendre	j'entends	nous entendons
to hear	*I hear*	*we hear*
	tu entends	vous entendez
	you hear	*you hear*
	il entend	ils entendent
	he hears	*you hear*

Si alors un enfant vient à vous, s'il rit, s'il a des cheveux d'or, s'il ne répond pas quand on l'interroge, vous devinerez bien qui il est.

Then, if a little man appears who laughs, who has golden hair and who refuses to answer questions, you will know who he is.

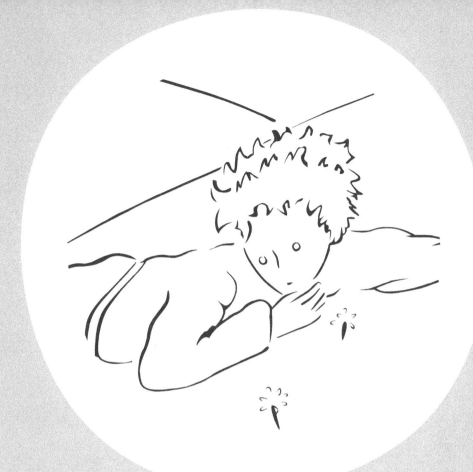

avoir to have	j'ai *I have*	nous avons *we have*
	tu as *you have*	vous avez *you have*
	il a *you have*	ils ont *they have*

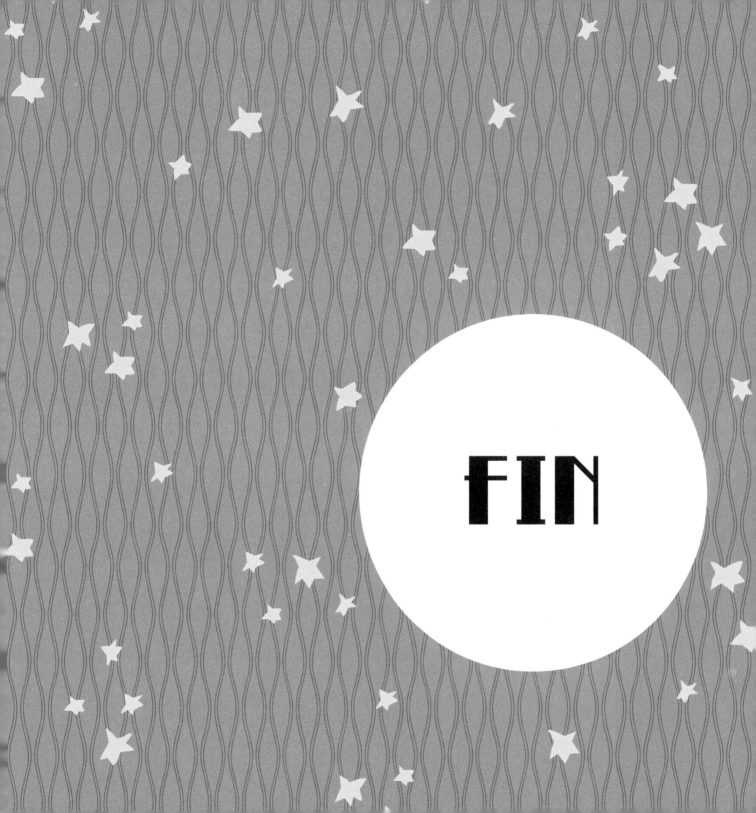

FIN

CPSIA information can be obtained
at www.ICGtesting.com
Printed in the USA
LVHW070747151220
673648LV00050B/311